THE 1970s

Sally Hewitt

W
FRANKLIN WATTS

This edition 2010

Franklin Watts
338 Euston Road
London NW1 3BH

Franklin Watts Australia
Level 17/207 Kent Street
Sydney, NSW 2000

Series editor: Sarah Peutrill
Series design: White Design
Art director: Jonathan Hair
Picture researcher: Diana Morris

A CIP catalogue record
for this book is available from
the British Library

ISBN: 978 0 7496 9630 6
Dewey number: 941'.0857

Printed in Malaysia

Franklin Watts is a division of
Hachette Children's Books,
an Hachette UK company.
www.hachette.co.uk

Picture credits:
AP/Topham: 4. Bettmann/Corbis: 11. Central Press/Hulton Archive:
17. Mary Evans PL: 10t, 13. Lynn Goldsmith/Corbis: 23t. Henry
Grant/Mary Evans PL: 16. Sally Greenhill/Sally & Richard Greenhill:
6b. Hulton-Deutsch Collection/Corbis: 20b. Colin Jones/Topham: 7.
Keystone/Hulton Archive: 14-15b, 29t. Kobal Collection: front cover drop-
in. Lucas Films/Kobal Collection: 24. Graham Morris/Evening Standard/Hulton Archive: front
cover b. Popperfoto: 27, 28b, 29b. Neal Preston/Corbis: front cover tl, 21. J. Pridmore/Popperfoto:
19. Science Museum, London/HIP: 12. Topham Picturepoint: 8, 9, 23b, 25, 26b. TRH Pictures: front
cover cr. UPPA.co.uk: 22b. Michael Webb/Keystone/Hulton Archive: 20t.

Whilst every attempt has been made to clear copyright should there be any inadvertent
omission please apply in the first instance to the publisher regarding rectification.

The author and publisher would like to thank everyone who contributed
their memories and personal photographs to this book.

Contents

Introduction

A TURBULENT TIME

In 1970 the voting age was lowered from 21 to 18, giving young people a say in politics for the first time. The 1970s, the first decade in which they could use their new power, was a time of political turbulence. In 1973, the price of oil rose bringing with it the threat of petrol shortages and causing the cost of living to go up all over the world. Britain suffered from inflation – a drop in the value of money.

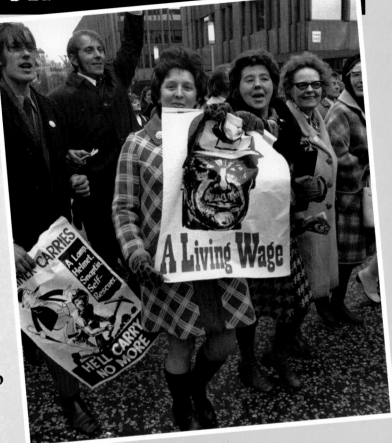

⬆ Miners' wives march in support of their husbands' claim for more pay.

STRIKES

In Britain, a series of strikes began that were to cause disruption and chaos. In 1973, a miners' strike led to a shortage of coal supplies to power stations. To save energy, the government introduced a three-day week. More strikes followed leading to the 'Winter of Discontent' in 1979 with rubbish left rotting in the streets and hospitals turning patients away.

LIFE STYLES

But the 1970s were not all bad. In general, people were able to enjoy more leisure time. Cheap package holidays meant that more people could afford to go abroad on holiday. Fast-food restaurants and new, imported ingredients changed the way that people ate. Colour televisions gradually replaced black-and-white televisions in the home.

MUSIC AND FASHION

Music and fashion defied the atmosphere of gloom. In the early 1970s, glam rock bands grew their hair, painted their faces and wore brightly-coloured, sparkling clothes. At the end of the decade, punk rock bands spiked their hair and wore studs and black leather in protest against the politicians.

BLOCKBUSTERS

Hugely successful films called blockbusters packed the cinemas with movie-goers. *Jaws*, the story of a man-eating shark, made a generation nervous of going into the water. Toys, stickers and posters based on the movie *Star Wars* filled the shops.

THEY CAN REMEMBER

In this book six people share their memories of what it was like to live in Britain in the 1970s. They each have a story to tell in their own section, but they also add other memories throughout the book.

Then

Now

Carole Cregeen

Carole lived in west London with her husband and children during the 1970s. She remembers what community life was like.

Sue Anderson

Sue describes growing up in the 1970s as the daughter of Jamaican immigrants. The IRA bombing campaign in London affected her in a very direct way.

Then

David Bedford

David grew up in Devon, and recalls some of his many childhood adventures.

Then

Now

Andrew King

Andrew lived in Bromley and was a fan of 1970s' music, especially glam and punk rock.

Now

Then

Helen Passey

Helen was at school and university during the 1970s. She remembers the strikes and the Winter of Discontent.

Nifa Vaz

Nifa came to Britain as a Ugandan refugee when she was nine years old.

Then

Now

Now

Carole Cregeen's story

Carole, 1971

⬇ Local police officers were well-known.

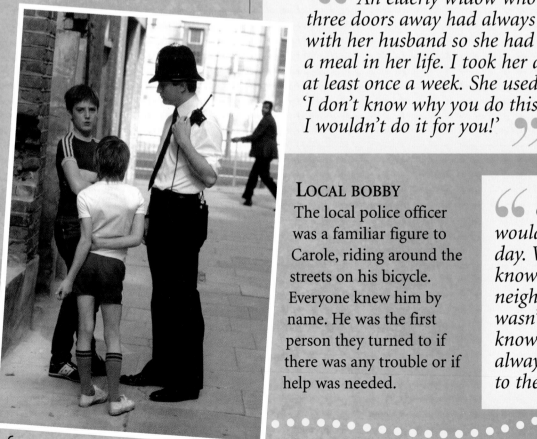

GOOD NEIGHBOURS

Carole and her husband Peter lived in a friendly community in west London. They had four children, Lucy, Maria and the twins, Tom and Emma. The children played outside in the street. Carole didn't worry about them. Neighbours always kept an eye on each others' children and made sure they were safe.

NEIGHBOURHOOD ASSOCIATION

Carole helped to set up a neighbourhood association in the 1970s that is still very active today. It involved shopping for those who couldn't get out, and driving people to hospital.

> " *An elderly widow who lived two or three doors away had always dined out with her husband so she had never cooked a meal in her life. I took her a cooked meal at least once a week. She used to say, 'I don't know why you do this for me. I wouldn't do it for you!'* "

LOCAL BOBBY

The local police officer was a familiar figure to Carole, riding around the streets on his bicycle. Everyone knew him by name. He was the first person they turned to if there was any trouble or if help was needed.

> " *Our local bobby would be there every day. What he didn't know about our neighbourhood wasn't worth knowing! He would always stop and chat to the children.* "

THE SILVER JUBILEE

In 1977, Queen Elizabeth II had been on the throne for 25 years. All over Britain bonfires were lit and street parties were held to celebrate her Silver Jubilee.

On Carole's street they decided to use the Silver Jubilee as a good excuse to get everyone together for a party. They asked the local police officer to help them get permission to close the road. When the day came, he joined the party too.

> We put up bunting [flags threaded onto string] and friends and family were all invited. In the afternoon we had games and fancy dress for the children followed by a traditional tea party with sandwiches, jelly, cakes and ice cream. In the evening we had an adult party with dancing to a steel band. Then the next morning, we had breakfast in the street as well.

! David remembers...

"I took unusually big newspapers into school with pictures of the Jubilee. We cut them out and made a scrapbook. We had photocopied sheets of the Crown Jewels which we cut out and coloured in."

A Silver Jubilee street party in Belfast, 1977.

MONEY TO SPEND

In general people had more money to spend than ever before. They spent more on their homes: painting their walls brown and orange, and installing baths in colours named after the new exotic foods you could buy in the shops, such as avocado and aubergine. They were also able to spend more money on going out and could have holidays abroad.

↑ Dark woods and the colour orange were popular in the 1970s.

NEW FOODS

Dinner parties became fashionable. People experimented with recipes from all over the world and tried out some of the new ingredients that became available in the shops – including garlic. Carole enjoyed experimenting with food.

> *I worked my way through a cookery book and cooked something new every day. We had lots of garlic and curries to get the children used to interesting food. We invited people for dinner and sat around in the kitchen talking into the small hours.*

! Andrew remembers...

"Our French teacher told us how to bite a clove of garlic and then swallow it quickly. That way, you didn't taste it but everyone else could smell it. The next day one of the boys bought along this bulb of garlic. We all tried it and the garlic did its magic. Two teachers that afternoon refused to teach us because of the smell!"

BABYSITTING

Carole remembers using the local babysitting rota so she could go out in the evening to the theatre and cinema with her husband.

> 66 *You had five points and lost one every time you went out. If you were out after midnight, you lost another point and another if you were out after 2 a.m. You gained a point when you babysat for someone else.* 99

Holidays

During the 1970s, package holidays offered cheap flights and accommodation in sunny places. Families who had always taken their holidays in Britain could now afford to go abroad. People set off for Spain's sandy beaches in their thousands, and also went on more adventurous holidays. Andrew and his family went to France in 1973.

"We stopped in a little French village for lunch but nothing was open except for this café that only had offal and tripe on the menu. Of course my brother and I wouldn't touch it. The old locals in the bar found the fact that we struggled with the food very amusing – which eventually, to our embarrassment, caused our father to stand up and sing the National Anthem at them in some sort of patriotic defiance!"

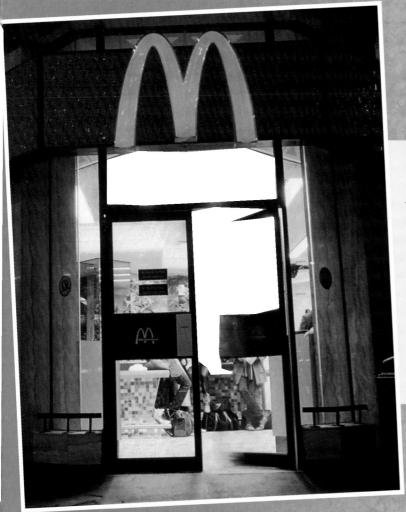

FAST-FOOD RESTAURANTS

Fast-food restaurants, such as Wimpey and McDonald's began to be opened all over the country. Andrew remembers the public's reaction.

> 66 *When McDonald's hit Bromley in the 1970s it was big news. It provoked a huge number of letters to the local newspaper about the downfall of society. My friends and I thought it was extremely exciting. We went to McDonald's when we went into Bromley on our own.* 99

← McDonald's still looks much the same today as it did in the 1970s.

David Bedford's story

David (middle), his brother Paul and sister Julie, 1977

GROWING UP IN DEVON

David and his brother Paul and sister Julie grew up in Braunton, Devon. The children roamed freely beyond the estate where they lived. They caught trout in the local stream, searched for brown crabs in the muddy estuary and slowworms in the fields. They had a lot of adventures.

↑ Fishing was a popular pastime for children living in the country in the 1970s.

GANGS

The children on David's estate belonged to different gangs. David's best friend in his gang was Trina.

David and Trina in fancy dress.

" Trina had a dog called Jenny – a black Labrador – who was born on the same day as Trina. Jenny protected us if we came across other gangs and there were things like stone-throwing. But really, it was just kids playing around. "

SKATEBOARDING

David's adventures often got him into trouble. One day he tried to recreate *Starsky and Hutch* – a popular American television series about two undercover police officers. Every episode featured high-speed car chases and daring stunts.

> *I was coming down the hill on my skateboard. My friends had parked their skateboards and I thought, wouldn't it be great – like* Starsky and Hutch – *to jump off my skateboard and land on another skateboard and zoom off down the hill. Of course, I woke up hours later on the settee. I'd been concussed for a couple of hours. We didn't have protective clothing or helmets.*

↓ Skateboard stunts took a great deal of practice.

RAID

One day, when David and his gang were bored, they planned a raid on a sweet shop.

> *It was like a jewelled grotto full of sweets we'd never had before. One at a time, we went in. I can't believe the shopkeepers didn't notice because we filled up a rucksack with sweets and went home with it on the back of a bike.*

GETTING CAUGHT

When David got home there was a knock on his door.

> *A police officer came in with his big hat on. I was frightened because he was very tall. He took his hat off, put it on the table and sat down. What he said has always stuck with me. He said – you're in trouble now, but you'll get out of trouble if you tell the truth. So we took the sweets back.*

A LESSON LEARNED

David never forgot the lesson he learned that night.

> *I'm glad it happened because I never got involved in serious trouble later on when I might have done.*

Childhood

AN ACTIVE CHILDHOOD

Without computer games to play with, and with only three television channels to watch, children were more likely to play outdoors in the 1970s. Chopper bikes, skateboards, pogo sticks and Spacehoppers were the toys every child longed for.

GREEN SHIELD STAMPS

Many of the toys were expensive, but if you couldn't afford them, Green Shield stamps could come to the rescue. Stamps were given to shoppers, depending on the amount they bought. When enough had been collected they could be exchanged for household items such as toasters, garden furniture and toys. David wanted a skateboard.

" My mum explained that we didn't have the money for skateboards. But our next-door neighbour worked in a garage where he was able to accumulate Green Shield stamps in huge amounts. He bought my brother and sister and me skateboards for Christmas with them. "

CHOPPER BIKES

Chopper bikes were popular with boys in the 1970s. David's gang used to ride them.

" All the boys had Chopper bikes. You could carry a passenger on the long saddle. They had a gear shift with a little knob like on a car. The knob nearly always came off leaving just a metal spike. If you stopped suddenly and skidded off the saddle you could do yourself an injury! They were great for doing wheelies. Some boys only ever rode their bike with the front wheel up in the air. "

↓ The Chopper bike had L-shaped seats and long handlebars.

AFTER SCHOOL

Nifa moved to Britain from Uganda in 1972. Her new life was different in many ways from her childhood in Uganda. She started to enjoy so many different activities that there wasn't much time left for homework.

> " *In Uganda, I got home from school, did my homework and read books. There wasn't much TV so I didn't get distracted by that.*
>
> *In England, I joined the choir, played netball, rounders and hockey – in fact I still play hockey now – I enjoyed all that. I watched TV. I used to watch* Blue Peter *and make all the things they showed.* "

➡ Bouncing around on a Spacehopper.

David remembers...
"*We had Spacehoppers. I remember their rubbery smell. Ours had a little smiley face. We used to just bounce around the garden holding the ears.*"

POCKET MONEY

Pocket money was usually just enough to buy a few treats on a Saturday morning. Carole gave pocket money to her children.

> " *The pocket money we gave our children was small compared with what children get now. It was a penny for every year of their life. But you could get quite a lot for a penny then.* "

Helen remembers...
"*Our local church had a youth club that was run by the curate. It used to attract local kids. We used to play snooker and I remember playing chess. It was fun and a focus for meeting other kids who weren't at the same school as me. There wasn't a great deal else to do and certainly nothing that didn't cost money.*"

Escape to Britain

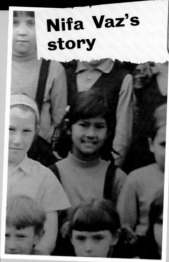

Nifa Vaz's story

Nifa, 1973

AMIN EXPELS ASIANS

In August 1972, Idi Amin, the military dictator of Uganda, a country in east Africa, announced that he planned to expel from the country all 50,000 Asians with British passports. Nifa was nine and living with her family in Uganda.

At the time, I didn't fully understand why we were being thrown out. I discovered much later that Amin asked the British government to loan him money. They said, 'We can't afford it and how are you going to pay it back?' So he decided to throw all the British Nationals out of the country.

48 HOURS' NOTICE

Suddenly, in September, the Asians were given 48 hours to leave Uganda. 30,000 went to Britain and 20,000 went to Canada, the USA and India. Nearly everyone arrived with very little money and few possessions. Nifa's mother had all her money taken from her at Uganda Airport.

We did get our stuff out because we just had ordinary things like pots and pans. Other families had their crates ransacked for valuables. When they arrived in Britain, they opened the crates and found they were full of stones.

MOVING TO LONDON

Camps were set up to receive the immigrants, but Nifa's family had a home to go to.

> 66 *My mother's cousin lived in Ealing, west London. He said – if you don't want to go to a camp, you can have my flat. He very generously moved out and lived with a friend. We had to cook and do everything in one room.* 99

↗ Nifa's mother's Girl Guide Company being inspected by Idi Amin in 1972, just before Amin expelled the Asians.

GIRL GUIDES

Nifa's mother had been a Girl Guide Commissioner in Uganda. Lady Gibbs, a British Girl Guide Commissioner, gave the family help and support when they arrived in London.

> 66 *The Girl Guides were very kind to us. Lady Gibbs took us to the theatre – to see* Treasure Island *which was wonderful because I had never seen live theatre.* 99

FINALLY SETTLED

After moving six times, the family finally settled down in Croydon and Nifa and her brother started going to school. Her mother worked as a supply teacher and her father found work in an office doing the accounts and book-keeping.

← An airlift was arranged to bring the Ugandan Asians to Stansted Airport in Britain.

Going to school

THE SCHOOL SYSTEM

At the beginning of the 1970s, most children went to one of three main kinds of state secondary school – grammar schools, technical schools and secondary modern schools.

GRAMMAR SCHOOL

To get into a grammar school, at the end of their primary schooling, pupils had to pass the Eleven Plus exam. If they failed it they would go to a technical school or secondary modern. Andrew passed his Eleven Plus.

I went to the local grammar school with some of my friends. I always felt it was a bit strange because a good friend of mine didn't get in. I thought this was ridiculous because as far as I was concerned he was as intelligent as everybody else.

I remember my first day in 1972. We all sat in the drama studio and the headteacher came in wearing a large gown. He swept in – it was almost like Batman coming in. His sheer presence made everyone sit up straight. One boy was so overwhelmed he burst into tears and had to go home.

⬇ A junior school classroom in the early 1970s.

COMPREHENSIVE SCHOOL

During the 1970s, comprehensive schools, introduced in the 1950s, at last largely replaced this system, and children no longer took the Eleven Plus or went to separate schools. Helen went to a comprehensive.

> " *There were large numbers of pupils at my comprehensive school in Chester who weren't interested in education. Sometimes they would jump out of the windows during lessons.* "

CALCULATORS

Calculators did not come into general use until the end of the 1970s, but Andrew remembers that there were other ways to do complicated calculations.

> " *When I first went to secondary school, we used a slide rule to do calculations. We also had calculating machines with levers. By the end of the 1970s, scientific calculators with many functions were easily available.* "

COMPUTERS

In the 1970s computers were only just coming into general use. Andrew remembers the first computer he ever used.

> " *There was only one computer in the whole of Bromley – in the town hall. We used to write out instructions for it on punch cards.* "

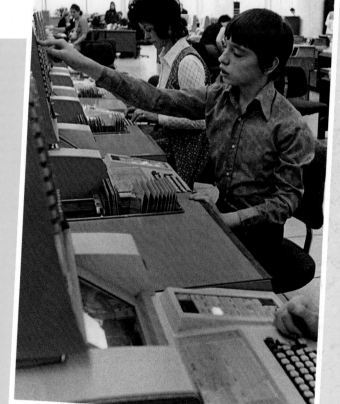

➡ A punch-card computer.

Different cultures

Sue Anderson's story

Sue, 1974

! Nifa remembers...

"*We started to get abuse in the area we were living in. There was one particular family who were openly not happy about us. They blocked the streets with their bicycles and wouldn't let us park. My mother said, 'I go to work and I pay my taxes. I'm going to call the police!' From then on, we weren't harassed.*"

GROWING UP IN WANDSWORTH

Sue's parents left Jamaica for a new life in Britain in the 1950s with their four children. Sue and her younger sister were born in London. When they were teenagers growing up in Wandsworth they were influenced by both Caribbean and British culture.

> *My dad said, 'While we are in England, act like the English people.' But my culture is Jamaican and I made it that way. Even though there were more black and Asian girls than English girls at my school, I had to learn about everyone else's culture and history. I had to search for information about my own. Now my children know just as much about black culture as they do about white culture.*

DOMINOES

Sue's dad played a Caribbean version of dominoes.

> *You slam the dominoes down. My mum's light bulbs used to shake when my dad and his friends were playing upstairs.*

➡ Sue (far right in both photos) and family, in the 1970s.

⬆ Revellers at the Notting Hill Carnival in 1979.

DISCIPLINE

Sue's father was a disciplinarian.

> 66 Dad was strict on us girls going out. At midnight, if we weren't back, he would lock the door. We had to go round to where my mum was working nights and she'd come home and shout at him to let us in. He didn't allow us to have boys around. 99

CARNIVAL

Sue started to go to the Notting Hill Carnival in the 1970s.

> 66 All the people who lived there used to sit outside and invite people in. They don't do it now. I followed the floats and danced the calypso. It was like a party on the street. 99

CARIBBEAN FOOD

Sue was brought up on Caribbean food, including fish, rice, beans, yams, plantain and coconut.

> 66 We never used to have English food when we were growing up – except fish and chips on a Friday. We always had proper Caribbean food. If Mum was working Dad would prepare it. 99

Sue now cooks Caribbean food for her family.

Fashion

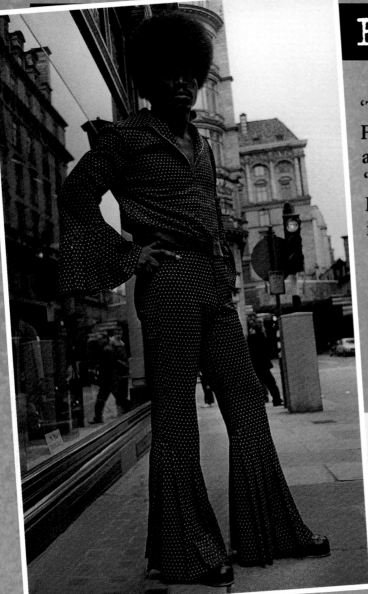

'THE DECADE THAT TASTE FORGOT'
Fashion in the 1970s was anything but subtle. It was called 'the decade that taste forgot'. Bright colours and stripes were in. Girls wore tiny miniskirts and even smaller shorts called hot pants. Everyone wore flares and sleeveless sweaters called tank tops. The more hair you had, the better.

Sue loved wearing the latest fashions.

> " *I had brown and cream tops with matching flares and a striped tank top. We had winged-collared shirts with big cuffs and platform shoes.* "

↑ Flared trousers and big Afro hair became popular.

Sue had fishnet tights, made with an open-meshed material.

→ Platform shoes were popular in the 1970s, with both men and women.

> " *I remember our budgie was flying around the room and he swooped down and got caught in my fishnet tights! He was pecking my leg and I was freaking out. My brothers were laughing.* "

HAIR

In the 1970s, having the right hairstyle was just as important as wearing the right clothes. Sue had Afro hair.

> **“** You could hide all kinds of things in your hair! I hid money in my Afro. One day I was combing my hair on the street without thinking anything about it. This police officer came up to me and said, 'That's a dangerous weapon.' I said, 'It's not, it's my Afro comb!' But after that, I bought one that you could fold like a fan. **”**

David was too young to worry much about what he wore, but he did worry about his hair.

> **“** I hated having my hair cut. I had a bowl cut – as long as I could have it. Once, the hairdresser came to our house and cut my hair very short. I wouldn't go out of the house until I saw she had been round to my friend's house and cut his even shorter. **”**

MAKE-UP

Sue's make-up was extravagant, too.

> **“** I wore loads of mascara so my eyelashes looked like broomsticks. I wore thick eyeliner. I looked as though I had black eyes. **”**

❗ Andrew remembers…

"The glam rock bands were wearing lots of very glittery clothes made of very shiny fabrics, with high heeled, ankle-length boots – stacks, as they were sometimes called. That's what you saw on TV but people didn't wear them really."

⬇ David Bowie brought a strange but glamorous style to the music stage in the early 1970s.

Music

Andrew, 1971

GLAM ROCK TO PUNK ROCK

Glam rock bands dominated the pop charts in the early 1970s. Then reggae bands (from Jamaica) and disco music got everyone dancing. Finally, punk rock bands upset the older generation with their angry political lyrics, studded jackets and spiky hair.

FIRST RECORD

Andrew can remember the first record he ever bought.

> *The first single I ever bought was 'Crazy Horses' by The Osmonds. I didn't realise there are some bands that girls liked and some bands that boys liked. So I was always a bit embarrassed about that – I'd bought a girl's record, for goodness sake!*

← American family pop group – The Osmonds. From left to right: Alan, Merill, Jay, Wayne, Donny and Jimmy.

! Sue remembers...

"I used to do all the disco dancing to 'Staying Alive' by the Bee Gees. We used to dance in a row – like line dancing – and all dance the same thing together. I went to a Bob Marley concert. I was a Michael Jackson fan when he was with the Jackson Five."

GLAM ROCK

Andrew was a big music fan all the way through the 1970s.

> *I got into glam rock when it was first happening. It just seemed so over the top. And of course my parents didn't like it and that made it all the more exciting.*

PUNK ROCK

When punk rock arrived on the scene in 1976, Andrew got into that too.

> " *Punk rock had a big influence on me. A lot of original punk bands, The Sex Pistols, Generation X and Siouxie and the Banshees, came from our area, Bromley. I loved the energy they put into their playing.* "

GUITAR HERO

Andrew took up the guitar and started to play in groups himself.

> " *I used to stand in front of the mirror and 'play' a tennis racket pretending to be a guitar hero, that I was in Slade. I do the same sort of pretending now.* "

Sometimes, Andrew's involvement with music clashed with his other interests.

> " *At the end of the 1970s the band I was playing in was asked to dress up like punks for an advert. I had to have pink hair. I couldn't get the dye out and I had to play in a chess tournament with pink hair.* "

Andrew still loves music and now plays in a glam rock tribute band.

↑ Sid Vicious, bass guitarist of one of the first punk bands – The Sex Pistols.

↓ Punk bands inspired a new look for young people.

Entertainment

Television, movies and hi-fis

Even though colour televisions were replacing black-and-white television sets during the 1970s, the cinema remained popular. A new kind of movie hit the screens – the blockbuster. Blockbusters appealed to everyone and made more money than movies had ever made before. There were no CDs in the 1970s but records on vinyl and cassette tapes were played on new hi-fi (high fidelity) players.

Don't go in the water

The first blockbuster was *Jaws*, made in 1975, about a man-eating great white shark. *Jaws* had a menacing catchphrase – 'Don't go in the water!' David was only eight when he went to see *Jaws* and he took the catchphrase to heart.

> ❝ *Whenever I heard the film's music I would say, 'He's coming! The shark's coming!' We lived near the beach and swam and played in the sea. I know there aren't great white sharks in the seas around Britain and I knew it then, but I'm still not very happy in the sea.* ❞

Star Wars

In 1977, everyone was going to see the latest blockbuster, *Star Wars*. It made even more money than *Jaws*. For the first time film-makers made toys of the characters from the film, which proved massively popular with children. David remembers the toys.

↑ In 1977 *Star Wars* broke box office money-making records.

> ❝ *Friends at school, especially the ones who were richer, collected* Star Wars *toys. We'd collected soccer stickers before, but not film merchandise.* ❞

GREASE

The music from the film *Grease* was as big a hit as the movie itself. Carole's daughter Lucy saw the film.

> " *Everyone was crazy about* Grease *at school – Olivia Newton-John with her spray-on trousers. It was the first album where I thought, ooh! I want to be like everyone else.* "

⬇ John Travolta and Olivia Newton John (centre) in *Grease.*

Television
• •

The biggest revolution for television was the widespread change to colour. At the beginning of the 1970s Andrew's family had a black-and-white television.

> *"My brother and I kept trying to persuade Dad that it would be much better if we had a colour TV to watch educational programmes like* Life on Earth *or* The Ascent of Man. *Eventually we got a colour TV in the mid 1970s."*

CASSETTE RECORDERS

Cassette recorders became more widely used in the 1970s, replacing less convenient, and more expensive reel-to-reel machines. Andrew got a portable cassette recorder for his 12th birthday.

> " *It was the big thing! I always remember my father telling me – you don't just have to listen to pop music on that.* "

Strikes and discontent

Helen, 1973

! Andrew remembers...

"I loved it. We had to have all these candles and it was really very exciting. At the time, I think we were less dependent on electricity than we are today.

THREE-DAY WEEK

During the early 1970s Britain's economy – the management of its money – was in trouble. People could buy less for their money. To make things worse, coal miners refused to work overtime. Coal for power stations was in short supply and this led to power cuts. In January 1974, in the middle of a cold winter, the Prime Minister, Edward Heath, called for a three-day week to save electricity. Helen was 16 in 1974. She remembers the effect the power cuts had on everyday life.

" *My parents looked in the local paper to see the times when the electricity would be off in our area. People were worried about basic things like whether their frozen food would stay frozen. We wore extra layers to keep warm and were allowed to wear our coats in school. I did my homework by candlelight.* "

Businesses were affected as well.

" *I had a Saturday job selling electrical equipment. I was attempting to sell washing machines and kettles with no power to plug them into. We weren't selling anything at all.* "

← People used candlelight during power-cuts.

WINTER OF DISCONTENT

Helen remembers the winter of 1978-79, which has now become known as the 'Winter of Discontent'.

⬆ Leicester Square in central London piled high with rubbish while refuse collectors went out on strike.

> " *I had just left university. It had been a very cold winter. All the public-sector unions had been on strike and no rubbish had been collected in London at all. Huge bin bags full of rubbish were piled up and Leicester Square was filled up with rubbish. It was really quite revolting.* "

DRIVING TEST

Helen found that the strikes affected everything, even her driving test.

> " *I was trying to organise a driving test and I simply couldn't do it because the people who would book you in were on strike and refusing to take bookings.* "

IRISH TROUBLES

In Northern Ireland, trouble was growing between the Republicans, who wanted Northern Ireland to become united with the rest of Ireland, and the Loyalists, who wanted to remain part of the UK. The IRA – the Irish Republican Army – attacked British forces in Northern Ireland. Then in 1971, it threatened to bomb mainland Britain.

BOMBING CAMPAIGN

The first attack was on an army barracks in Aldershot in Hampshire. A car bomb exploded killing seven civilians. After that, the bombing campaign spread to the whole of the country and continued throughout the 1970s.

In 1973, Sue was working as a hairdresser in Selfridges, a department store in London, when an IRA bomb went off and destroyed the ground floor.

> *" I was working in the salon on the first floor. All of a sudden the whole building shook and glass broke and people were screaming and shouting. The ladies were running around with rollers in their hair. I was really, really scared. My parents were worried. There were no mobile phones to tell your family what had happened. It didn't really hit me until I got home and saw it on the TV and my mum burst out crying. "*

← A view through a shattered window opposite the Selfridges building, the day after the bomb. Amazingly only a few people were slightly injured.

Important changes

Decimalisation

In 1971, Britain copied other European countries to make its currency decimal. The old system of 12 pence to a shilling and 20 shillings to a pound became 100 new pence to a pound. It was much simpler, but people still grumbled about making the change.

European Economic Community

In January 1973 Britain, Ireland, Denmark and Norway joined France, Italy, West Germany, Belgium, Luxembourg and the Netherlands in the EEC – the European Economic Community. This meant that the population of the EEC was now bigger than that of the United States.

⬆ It took a while for people to get used to the new system of currency.

FIRST WOMAN PRIME MINISTER

The voting age had been lowered from 21 to 18 in 1970. Helen had just missed being able to vote in 1974, but in 1979, at last, she had her first chance to vote. She felt that it was an important election.

The Conservatives won the general election and Margaret Thatcher became the first British woman prime minister. People looked forward to the 1980s with renewed hope that the economy's troubles were behind them.

> ❝ The Labour Government had been in for five years. There had been non-stop strikes during the whole of that period. I think people had become fed up with a government that couldn't control the public-sector unions. ❞

⬅ Margaret Thatcher waves to well-wishers outside 10 Downing Street, on her first day as prime minister.

Timeline

1970
1st January The British voting age is lowered from 21 to 18.
19th June Conservatives win election. Edward Heath becomes prime minister.

1971
9th February First British soldier killed in Northern Ireland.
15th February Decimal currency is introduced.

1972
22nd January Britain joins the European Economic Community.
30th January British troops kill 13 civilian demonstrators in Londonderry, Northern Ireland, in what became known as 'Bloody Sunday'.
21st September Asians with British passports are expelled from Uganda by dictator Idi Amin.

1973
3rd March One person killed and 250 injured in IRA bomb attacks on London.

1974
January Miners' overtime ban forces government to introduce a three-day week.
8th August President Nixon of America resigns after the Watergate scandal.
11th October Labour wins the general election with a majority of three seats. Harold Wilson becomes prime minister.
21st November 17 people are killed in Birmingham pubs by an IRA bomb.

1975
11th February Margaret Thatcher replaces Edward Heath as leader of the Conservative Party.
3rd October The Queen opens North Sea oil pipeline bringing oil to Britain.

1976
21st January The first passenger flights of two Concorde supersonic jet airliners, from London to Bahrain and from Paris to Rio de Janeiro.
August Water rationing is introduced during the driest summer of the century.

1977
7th June The Queen opens a week of festivities to celebrate her Silver Jubilee.

1978
26th July The first test-tube baby is born in Britain.

1979
January The streets are filled with rubbish during the 'Winter of Discontent'.
4th May Conservatives win the election. Margaret Thatcher becomes the first female British prime minister.

Glossary

Bowl cut A kind of hair cut that looks as though a bowl has been put on someone's head and the hair left showing has been cut off.

Calypso A Caribbean song with an off-beat (syncopated) rhythm.

Commissioner Someone who represents and works for an organisation or a country.

Community The people who live and work together in a neighbourhood.

Culture The art, music, ideas and beliefs of a particular society.

Curate An assistant clergyman in the Church of England.

Dictator A leader who rules a country with total authority.

Disciplinarian Someone who believes in enforcing strict rules.

Discontent A feeling of unhappiness or dissatisfaction.

Exotic A word that describes unfamiliar things from a foreign country.

Generation People within a certain age group. Teenagers are from a younger generation than their parents.

Immigrant Someone who leaves the country they were born in to make a new life in another country.

Inflation The way money loses its value and becomes worth less than before.

Merchandise Things for sale. Film merchandise is such things as toys and games based on the characters in a film.

Neighbourhood The area that surrounds the place where you live.

Overtime Extra time spent working outside regular work hours.

Package holiday A holiday arranged by a tour company that includes travel and somewhere to stay.

Public sector Services paid for by the tax payer such as hospitals, schools, fire stations and refuse collection.

Reel-to-reel A kind of tape recorder where the tape runs from one wheel, called a reel, to another.

Slide rule A calculator that looks like a ruler. Calculations are made by sliding two mathematic scales against each other.

Society A group of people that live and work together and share a way of life.

Strike When workers refuse to work because they are in dispute with their employers over pay or other issues.

Union An organisation that represents and stands up for the rights of groups of workers.

Index